On Spirit Wings

Ann Patterson

Spirit Wings Publishing
www.spiritwings.info

Typeset in Giovani and printed in Altona, Manitoba, Canada by Friesens

First Priniting: June 2002

National Library of Canada Cataloguing in Publication Data
Patterson, Ann, 1947-
On spirit wings
Poems.
ISBN 0-9730454-0-X

I. Title.
PS8581.A78587O5 2002 C811'.6 C2002-901095-0
PR9199.4.P38O5 2002

Photographer: Trevor Mills
Editor: Bernard Shalka
Book and Cover Design: Leon Phillips www.leonphillips.ca

Dedication

This book is dedicated to Keith and Sarah, my children, for their support and love and for choosing to share their lives with me. It is dedicated to my parents for their guidance throughout the years, and to the memory of my husband Mark, my best friend for thirty years. It is thanks to him that this process began. Thank you also to Holly Fourchalk for being my friend and for teaching me to meditate and to Robert Currie, who brought joy and light back into my life if only for a few brief moments. A big thank you to all the people at the Atlin Creativity Retreat in June 1998, especially to Kate Collie and Graham Good who taught me to look intently at the world around me and to write haiku. I especially want to thank my teachers at Capilano College for their encouragement and training: Nancy Boyd, painting and drawing; Wayne Eastcot and Steven Dixon, printmaking; and Pierre Coupey, writing. I owe a huge debt of gratitude to Trevor Mills for his many hours spent photographing my artwork. Thank you also to Grant Gaudet for his help, ideas, and his encouragement. Also to Jorge Rocha at Friesens for his help, to Bernard Shalka for his editing skills, and to Leon Phillips for his wonderful design ideas. You are the people who made this book possible. I am extremely grateful for your support.

Contents

10 *Preface*

14/15 Opening/*Prayer*
16/17 *Prayer*/Joyful
18/19 Emerging Depths/*Elegy*
20/21 *The Floods*/Rot Can Be Beautiful
22/23 Dancing Flowers/*The Dance*
24/25 *In Dreams*/In Dreams
26/27 Out of Time/*Out of Time*
28/29 Depression/*Depression*
30/31 Release and Clearing/*Release* and *Clearing*
32/33 Accept the Moment/*Accept the Moment*
34/35 Experience/*Experience*

Contents

Joy/*Joy* 36/37

On a Mountainside/Travels 38/39

Knowing/*Medicine Wheel* 40/41

Seeing/*Open Your Senses* 42/43

Seeds for Thought/*Pine Cones* 44/45

Wild Roses/Wild Roses 46/47

Tide is Out/*Atlin Lake* 48/49

Lupine Drops/Rising 50/51

The Fungus Fairy/*Carol and Me* 52/53

The Artist/The Goddess 54/55

The Crossing/*The Christ* 56/57

Thank You/River's Turning 58/59

Her Pain/*Be Careful What You Ask For* 60/61

Contents

62/63 *His Pain*/His Pain

64/65 Mystic Forest Box/*The Mystic Forest Path*

66/67 *Treasures*/Our Fears Are Dragons

68/69 Comfort/*A Moment in Time*

70/71 *Metamorphosis*/Transformation

72/73 Spirit Wings/*Spirit Wings*

74/75 *Prayer*/Spirit Connections

76/77 She Brings Forth Fruit/*Collection*

78/79 *The Fall*/Spirit Pool

80/81 *The Web of Life*/Web of Life

82/83 Connected/*Prayer*

84/85 A Collection/*Atlin*

Contents

Inspiration/*Reverence* 86/87

Treasures/*The Collector* 88/89

Morning Reflections/Tide Pool Revisited 90/91

Reflections/*Reflections* 92/93

Low Tide/*Waking* 94/95

Spirit Wings 2/*Dusk* 96/97

Night/The Navy Mountain 98/99

Hope/*Skybright* 100/101

Sheltered/Sheltered 102/103

The Heart of the Matter/*My Wish For You* 104/105

About the Works 106

Preface

The act of defining oneself is usually a hidden process, especially to the person involved. Each action, each word, each thought in life helps to determine the future thoughts and attitudes of the person. Step by step we each create ourselves, slowly evolving, mostly unaware. At some point a period of intense disquiet or overwhelming grief may occur. Out of this time, awareness may start to dawn for the person. One begins to become aware of the ability to create ourselves, to better understand our connection to others, and to see life as a process. Out of numbness and blackness new questions arise. What is my purpose? Who am I? Who do I want to be?

Why is it that we go through a period of blackness before the dawning of the light? Must we uncreate ourselves, significantly disturb our so tightly entrenched beliefs, bring these beliefs of which we are mostly unaware into our consciousness before we can change, before we can admit we can't do it alone and learn to surrender to the Infinite?

Once we start to ask these questions there may be sudden leaps of insight when we see with clarity and vision, and our inner lives change at a tremendous rate. There will likely also be times when we seem to have lost the ability to be aware, to be connected, and we feel at a standstill. Perhaps we're just resting, cocooning, integrating, consolidating what we have learned, a time of taking our new awareness of heart and mind and practising it in the world. These are the times when we learn patience and trust. We learn to appreciate that life is a never-ending process. We never arrive but are continually evolving.

Slowly we learn to appreciate all aspects of ourselves, even those we have formerly thought of as negative, perhaps whose existence we have even denied. As we learn to appreciate ourselves, our compassion and understanding for others grows and our connection to the Universal Spirit grows stronger.

We also learn to honour our dreams and to define our acts of power. It is through the conscious decision to spend our time and efforts on a chosen task that we create ourselves, that we hone our courage.

That is what I am doing with this book. Out of depression and grief has arisen a longing for life, love, light, joy, and expansion—a longing to know and to create my purpose in life. A longing to make a difference.

And so I have chosen to learn new things, to set aside my fears, to expand my awareness and my horizons.

I hope this collection of poems, prayers, and art work will touch you in places you need to be touched and will help to expand your awareness of yourself, your capabilities, your love for life, and your connection to the Infinite.

Opening, watercolour on paper, 5 x 9⅛", 2000

There is only one Source, one Creator, and this one is Spirit. I know and accept that I am an important, worthy, loving, lovable, and valuable part of this One. Spirit wants and needs me to express my uniqueness, joy, creativity, and love. I direct these into all my activities. This day I choose to live from this knowledge and to open myself to receive abundant goodness and love. I am a person who creates all I want and need through my faith in the generosity of Spirit. And so it is.

November 1997

Prayer

There is only one Source, one Creator, and this one is Spirit. I am an individualised expression of this One, created in its image.

I am the creator of my life and with Spirit's help a co-creator of the Universe. I create my life through my thoughts, words, and actions. I choose to create a full, loving, vibrant, passionate, joyful, healthful, helpful life. Each day I watch my creation (myself) unfold and experience it fully.

I am a playful and loving spirit. My life and work are filled with these qualities. My eyes, face, and body sparkle because I'm filled with vitality, curiosity, creativity, humour, joy, love, and light. My body, mind, and spirit are healthy, relaxed, and at peace. I love life and it loves me. I look forward with enthusiasm to each new day. I am kind, compassionate, and patient with myself and with all others. I easily release judgments because I see all sides of an issue with ease. I know that we are all perfectly imperfect. I know that there is nothing to fear and so I release fears from the past easily and joyfully. I am good enough and have always been so. I am confident, capable, strong, courageous, and resilient. I am truly grateful for my life, for all I have, for all that I experience, for all my opportunities, and all that I am. And so it is.

January 1998

Joyful, oil monotype print, 8½ x 12", 1998

Emerging Depths, fabric, 11 x 13″, 2001

Elegy

I do not look for him
in my bed,
nor at the breakfast table.

He was not at his daughter's wedding
nor his father's bedside at his ending.

He is not there when the roof
starts to leak
nor when appliances
break and bend.

But all is not lost. He can still be found
atop that mountain peak
and in the ripples of the stream
where I walk.

His words come to me on gentle breezes
and when the trees bend and sway.

He gently rocks me upon ocean waters
and feels my tears in each rainfall,
but only in my dreams
can I be held at all.

The Floods

The roof leaks
soaking wood and carpet.
Appliances held together
by shoe string
let go.
The kitchen flooring heaves
like ocean waves in the deluge.
The shower leaks,
sending rivulets of water
to the floor below.
Drains clog and the basement
floods,
mildews and fills with mould.

All is broken down,
so fast, so fast,
upon your leaving.

Rot Can Be Beautiful, watercolour on paper, 6 3/8 x 9 1/8", 2000

Dancing Flowers, acrylic and mixed media on panel, 24 1/8 x 18 1/8", 2000

The Dance

Dying flowers dance
shaking new life in the
winds—
last glorious act.

Breath of new life springs
continuously reborn
from the dying dance.

In Dreams

In dreams I walk with you.
In dreams I talk with you.
In dreams you hold me.
In dreams you enfold me.
In dreams I listen.

In Dreams, acrylic and mixed media on panel, 21⅛ x 16½", 1999

$1.50
New Zealand
$1.50
$1.00
New Zealand
New Zealand
New Zealand
New Zealand
IN DREAMS
world

Out of Time, acrylic and mixed media on panel, 20 3/8 x 16 1/2", 2000

Through tears pressing lids
she sees

a rhodo
in the shelter of vine maples,
flowering sparsely.
It will feel the winter kill
for blooming
out of time.

Depression, acrylic and mixed media on panel, 16⅜ x 10⅞", 1999

Numbed to the bone
constricted mind, heart tight and
devoid of feeling.

Hurt descends again
I've felt the black emptiness
been scorched by life.

Release and Clearing, acrylic and mixed media on panel, 16 5/8 x 10 7/8", 1999

Release

Body release this pain
this tightness of joints and soul.
Let the clear air in.

Clearing

Warm tears pour freely
cleansing heart, mind, and spirit.
Release with pain.

Accept the Moment, acrylic and mixed media on panel, 16⅝ x 10⅞″, 1999

Surrender myself
to all experiences.
Accept the moment.

Experience, acrylic and mixed media on panel, 16⁵⁄₈ x 10⁷⁄₈″, 1999

Strong warm wind buffets,
shaking loose misconceptions,
exposing essence.

The I Am that remains
experiences herself
moment by moment.

Joy, acrylic and mixed media on panel, 16⅝ x 10⅞″, 1999

Filled with its presence
I feel warm, magical, open,
ever expanding, never ending.
It is a lightness of heart,
a deep heartfelt happiness
filled with wonder and magic.

On a Mountainside

Wind rushes through me
cleansing the spaces within,
making me wholly me.

Medicine Wheel

Up on the mountain
searching for my space,
eagle wheels high above me.
This then is my place.

Stones guard and connect.
This sacred space protects.

Inviting guidance
to this hallowed site,
energy of earth called forth
bring me clarity and light.

Lessons to be learned
from sun, rain, and lake,
east, west, above and below,
make no mistake.

Grant me insights clear and real—
oh, my medicine wheel.

Seeing, photoetch print, 11⅞ x 11⅞", 1999

Open your ears,
your eyes.
Respond with all your senses.
Let the process
 create
 you.

One with moon, with lake,
merge with
sky
sun
air
the earth around you.

Seeds for Thought, photoetch print, 11⅞ x 11⅞", 1999

Wombs pregnant with life
hold the next generation
waiting to be born.

Wild Roses

Pungent sweetness found
as nose caresses petal,
rose scent filling me.

Wild Roses, acrylic and mixed media on panel, 24 1/8 x 18 1/4", 2000

Tide is Out, intaglio etching, 9 x 11⅞", 1998

Atlin Lake

Twinkling waters,
shimmering stars of clear light
pierced my heart with blue.

Lupine Drops

Raindrops,
rare diamonds discovered
after the storm.
Liquid jewels
cradled in lupine fronds.
Some drops small, some large,
all perfectly perfect.

Rising, oil monotype print, $8^{1}/_{2}$ x $14^{1}/_{16}$", 1998

The Fungus Fairy, watercolour on paper, 11 x 14 3/4", 2000

Discovered when
climbing into a painting
truths before unknown.
Sharing experiences
then finding we are one.

The Artist

A stiff leathery sun-darkened hand
brushes across the canvas page
spreading swatches of colour,
precise patches of green, blue, ochre on white.
Eyes search, work to decipher
each nuance of tone.
Eyes blink, light changes,
another colour, another pattern emerges.

Dry scratches, fluid watery colours
caress and claw the page.
Joyous upswelling, bubbling free,
then rage displayed—
hellish search for truth.
Emotions written in tempera.

Each stroke a search,
always looking,
looking for the light
inside as well as out.

Where are the shadows?
What colours are they?
Greens, lapis, violets?
Carnelian perhaps?
Colour delights the senses,
filling and drowning them.

Intensity, attention
given to each small detail.
Looking for the Now,
never able to portray it.
That instant now past.

A new way of seeing wells up.
Feel the colours.
Breathe them.
Feel the light—
let it wash through the body.
Then paint how it feels.
Each stroke the truth of now.

The Goddess, acrylic and mixed media on panel, 15 x 18", 2000

The Crossing, acrylic and mixed media on panel, 10 7/8 x 13 5/8", 2002

The Christ

I have a Christ in the wall
above my bathtub.
How many can say they too
have a Christ in their wall above their
bathtub? Not many
I should think.
But mine has been there for three years
and more.
How it got there I do not know.
It wasn't there for the twenty
years before, but came
at a time of need.

I get great pleasure lying
in my tub.
I snuggle into the warmth and
watch this holiness.
His body is a golden hue with arms
upstretched.

Small dark patches pierce where
his hands would be. I can not see
his eyes, but the light
around his head extends
far up the wall.

He usually faces left,
his left ankle crossing his right,
but on some nights
the rings defining his muscles
face the other way, making
him appear
more gaunt.

He is my secret treasure found
not below but above
the lion, that beautiful woman
and the Indian mask.

Thank you

The room burst into stars
when I first met you.
Blinded by the light, I was magically
magnetically pulled towards you.
Obsessed from the start
I could not resist your laughter,
your wit,
or your smiling golden eyes.

You listened and I felt heard.
Seduced by your kisses
my senses reeled,
opened as never before.
You brought joy and sunlight into my life.
I asked and Spirit brought you,
then took you again.

River's Turning, watercolour on paper, 13⅝ x 10", 1998

Her Pain, oil monotype print, 11½ x 9⅞", 1998

Be Careful What You Ask For

I tried to take on your pain,
I thought I could make a difference.
I begged and pleaded with Spirit,
hoping to help just a little.

Spirit granted me my wish
in ways I had not expected,
because when you left
I got more pain
than I had ever known existed.

I tried to learn the lessons,
appreciate the gifts given,
but still the pain was strong,
so strong. Endless.

At last I realised I could never
take on your pain.
It was not to share,
but yours alone to bear.

In my asking all I had done
was increase my own.

His Pain

Soul screams
lies, lies, lies.
World crumbles.
Twice accused.
Rage and scream
unfair, unfair!
Hot tears scorch throat,
gouge cheeks.
Totally destroyed?

Accident upon accident
intended or not?
Who knows? I do.
Pain cries, slow down, slow down.
Continual pain in the back
and in the heart.

Hold onto the pain.
Keep it safe. Keep it clear,
untouched.

Push to experience all;
danger beckons.
Need excitement to feel alive,
powerful, skillful, strong.
Adrenaline rush! Must keep doing.
If I stop
I might have to think,
to feel.
If I did would there be
any me left
or final disintegration?

His Pain, monoprint, $9\frac{1}{8}$ x $11\frac{7}{8}$", 1998

Mystic Forest Box, assemblage, 18 x 14¼", 1999

The Mystic Forest Path

Wild sweet roses hide beneath the pines,
blanketing slopes with pink and rose.
Their scent upon the wind.

Heather creeps and twinflower leaves glisten
among firs with needles soft and warm.
The roses here a more vivid hue.

Further on blackcurrants form their fruit in a bluebell patch
that's sprinkled with lupines.
A spot that will soon sport delphinium blooms.

White bunchberries cloak the mossy forest floor,
bluebells, arnicas yellow and bright.
Orange columbines spring forth
in hidden glades few will see.

More bunchberry snow
beside the cone and needle path.
Filtered sun caresses each white bloom.
A place to pause and wonder
mysterious mystic forest path.

Treasures

Our fears are dragons guarding our deepest treasures.
Do we dare to look them in the eye?

What do you fear?
Failure—palpitations, churning knotted gut,
clenched teeth, or success too easily gotten?

Perhaps you don't measure up
(in whose eyes?)
or are you cast aside—
derelict, forlorn, forsaken, forgotten?

Pain sears and rips squashing chest and gut.
It may immobilise and numb.

Can you get past the flames and the anger
to find what you might learn?

Dig. Dig.
Wade through the muck to find,
to dust and clean and polish yourself.

More sweet for all the work.

Our Fears Are Dragons, watercolour on paper, $5\frac{3}{4}$ x $9\frac{1}{8}$", 2000

Comfort, oil monotype print, 12 x 13 3/8″, 1998

He came and he went
without the slightest intent
of staying.

He gave a little
and he took even less,
wrapped up as he was
in his own distress.

But still his arms
were warm and comforting.

Metamorphosis

The transformation begins
slowly at first,
changes deep within,
hidden from the light.

Darkest depression
born in numbness black and cold.
Is this a requirement for change?

How much darkness is enough
before the worm of pain fattens
and expands,
creating a crack of light,
a streak of hope,
a moment of joy?

Rest again, renew, regenerate—
quiet peaceful time.
But under the surface
change continues.
Until at last the wing colours
begin to show.

A thunderous rent,
new wings emerge—
life forever changed,
more delicate, more beautiful
than before—

a life reborn.

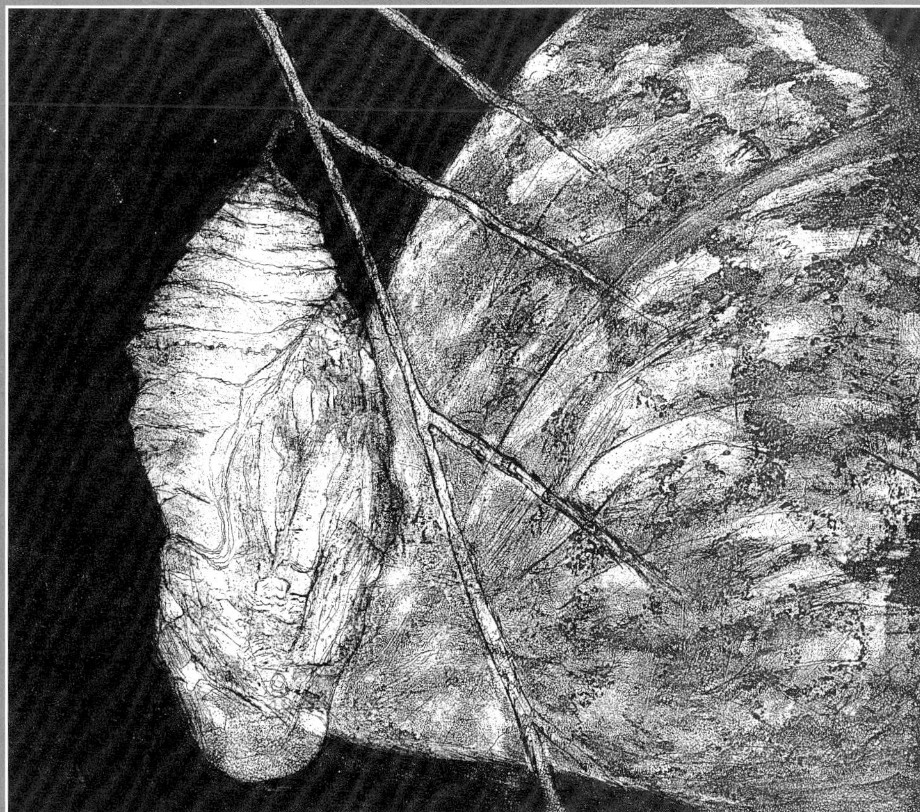

Transformation, intaglio etching, 13½ x 11½″, 1998

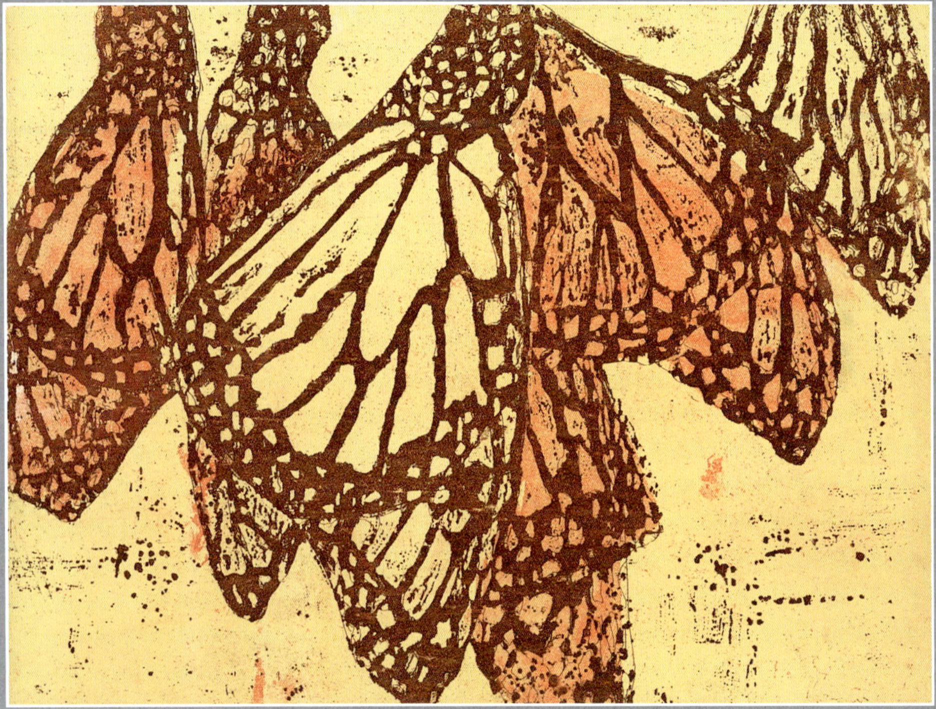

Spirit Wings, intaglio etching, 12⅛ x 9″, 1998

Gossamer wings
delight the senses.
Sparkling jewels of
orange and gold,
harbingers of
joy and change.

There is only one Source, one Creator, and this one is Spirit. I am always good enough because Spirit created me from the Universal essence—Love.

All I need is always provided by Spirit. I am open and receptive to abundance and prosperity in my life. I am open to giving and receiving love and to having ever more loving relationships. Others' choices are their business, they in no way impact upon whether I am worthy or lovable.

I know that there are no wrong turns, no mistakes, so I look for the lessons, the gifts, and for the joy in each moment. I am grateful for this knowing, for my life, for my body, for my work, for my relationships, and for the knowledge that I am always loved by Spirit and am one with all. I trust that there is even better yet to come. And so it is.

July 1998

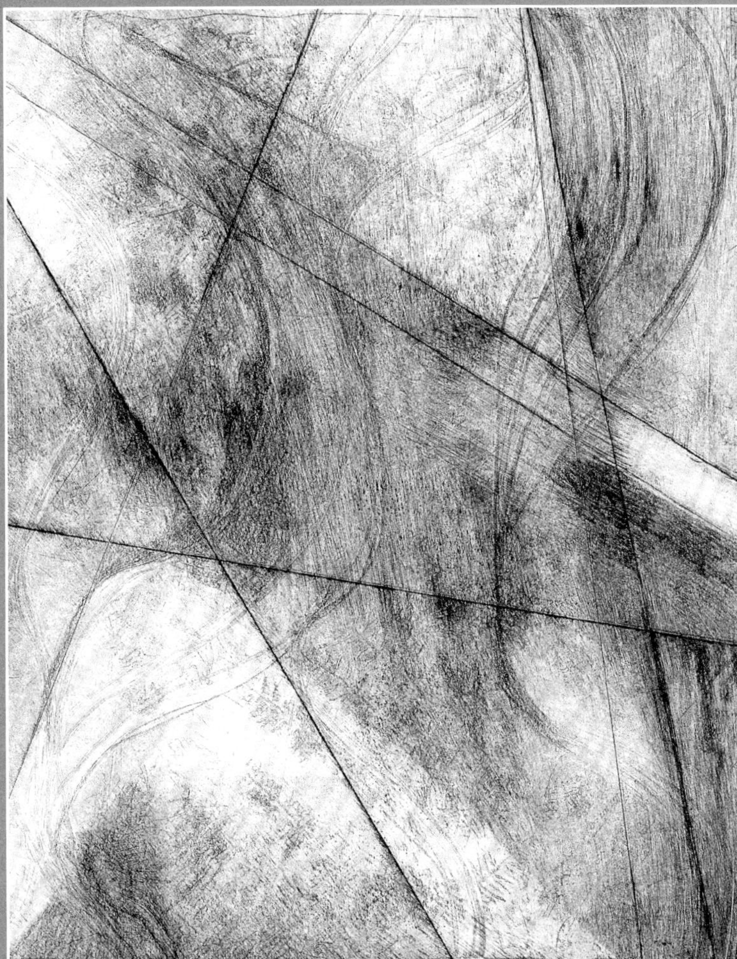

Spirit Connections, intaglio etching, 9⅝ x 12″, 1997

She Brings Forth Fruit, acrylic and mixed media on panel, 15 x 18⅛", 2000

I am a collector,
a hoarder of pains
stored in twisted spine
and tightened muscle,

holding fast to each feeling,
each image, each doing.
Then
fighting

to break free,
to release
the collection.

The Fall

Brittle
crackling
luminous beings
leap, skip,
twirl,
and dance in the streets.

Most magnificent
in their closure.

Releasing
suppleness
and constraints,
they crumble
to dust.

Spirit Pool, intaglio print, 9 x 5⅞", 1998

The Web of Life

The web of life,
a tangled weave of paths and branches.
Each path leads towards our goal.

A circuitous route
(tortuous? perhaps.)
filled with pains and joys,
each choice slowly leads us on.

Slowly the questions come
and slowly are answered.
Is it age or pain that brings the questions?
Or only makes them more relevant?
Who am I? Where am I going?
What is my truth?
What is my purpose?
Am I loved? Am I alone?
Is there a God? Why?
Why am I here?

The truth is I am alone—
alone in birth, in death,
in my thoughts and feelings.
Yet part of all creation.
A relevant part.

My challenge is to love,
especially when it is difficult,
for I impact and change
each person I meet
with my deeds and words,
and I am changed by them.
Each one a miraculous part
of the whole, connected to all.

It is this need to share love,
to feel love,
to be loving
that we are here to learn.

Web of Life, acrylic and mixed media on panel, 24 x 18", 2000

Connected, watercolour on paper, 11¼ x 15¼", 2000

There is only one Source, one Creator, and this one is Spirit. All of the powers of Spirit are within me and are mine to use. I am aware that I am using these creative powers each day and am grateful for this knowledge.

My senses are open and receptive to the beauty and truth within me and around me, and I appreciate both. I am "aware" of what is right for me, of what my intuition is telling me at all times, and I act on this knowledge. Because this is so, I treat myself with gentleness, love, and patience. I feed my body nourishing foods. I get enough exercise and rest. I listen to my body, mind, and spirit so I ask what I need to ask of others and express what I need to express to them easily, joyfully, compassionately, and clearly. My relationships with my family and friends improve each day. I allow new people, new friendships into my life.

I surrender to Spirit and am thankful for all the goodness in my life. And so it is.

December 1998

A Collection, photoetch print, 11 7/8 x 11 7/8", 1999

These past days have been a collection,
a collection of connections;
like the green beads of twinflower leaves
that cascade over the banks.
A collection of stones—
some lined with river veins,
others marked with an unknown language.
Still others dressed in vibrant lichen blazes—
beach stones, mountain stones.
A collection of beach twigs—
twisted knurled beauty.
A collection of flowers
in the picking
and in the seeing and naming.
New ones just waiting to be known.
A collection of sounds—
bird, wind, human, mosquito,
mouse scratchings and squeaks.
A list of critters encountered.
A collection of scents—
aspen, wild rose, bedstraw,
smoke, incense.
A collection of days
and of footsteps taken.
A collection of pains revisited
and newly known.
A collection of tears, of laughter,
of unnameable emotions.
Collections of words, poems,
paintings, and colours.
A collection of shimmers—
quaking aspen leaves,
sparkling light on pond
and lake.
Still more of raindrops,
sundrops, dragonflies,
butterflies, lichen, pinecones.
A collection of vistas—
of broad expanses,
of seeing clearly into forever.
A collection of attention paid
to the minute,
to the moment.
A collection of insights,
of prayers and celebrations.
A collection of friends
and of gifts shared.
Atlin.

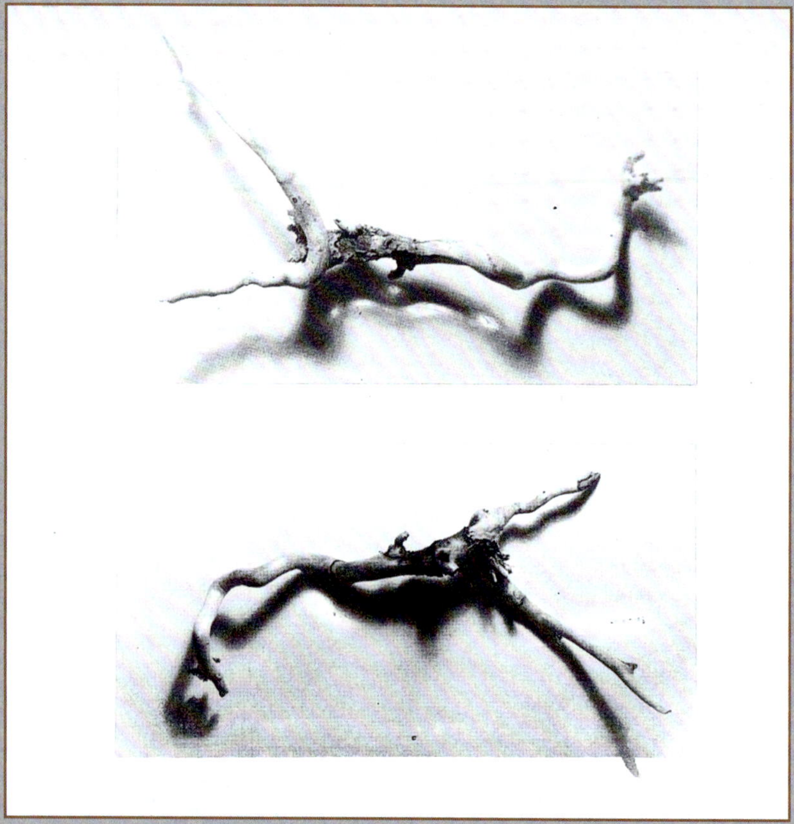

Inspiration, photoetch print, $11\frac{7}{8}$ x $11\frac{7}{8}$", 1999

Reverence is the deep awareness
of the value of a thing
and great gratitude
for its existence.

It is the respectful honouring
of the thing,
blessing it and being blessed
through knowing it.

Treasures, photoetch print, 11 7/8 x 11 7/8″, 1999

Wings beat the air,
as chickadees whirr
and compete for
black
berries.

Fragrant juice
stains hands and lips.
Sweetness,
punctuated by mind
puckering
sour.

She ambles the trail,
leaves scrunching
underfoot.

A fallen lichen
from a nearby alder,
cool and spongy—
in the hand,
palest
green.

Leaves give way now
to looser
gravel.

Seed pods sway
on the sunny slope,
foxgloves
turned to wood.

Waxy white fruits form
amid the ones
that forgot to ripen;
poisonous
snow
berries.

Purple fingers
at path's end
still clutch seed cases
and lichen,
crusty dry
but warmer
now.

Morning Reflections

Greens and
golds
ripple.

Umbers and tans
slice through
swaying
water.

Black holes
pierce
the surface
mirror—

copies of
deeper shadows.

Tide Pool Revisited, intaglio and deep etch print, 12 x 8", 1997

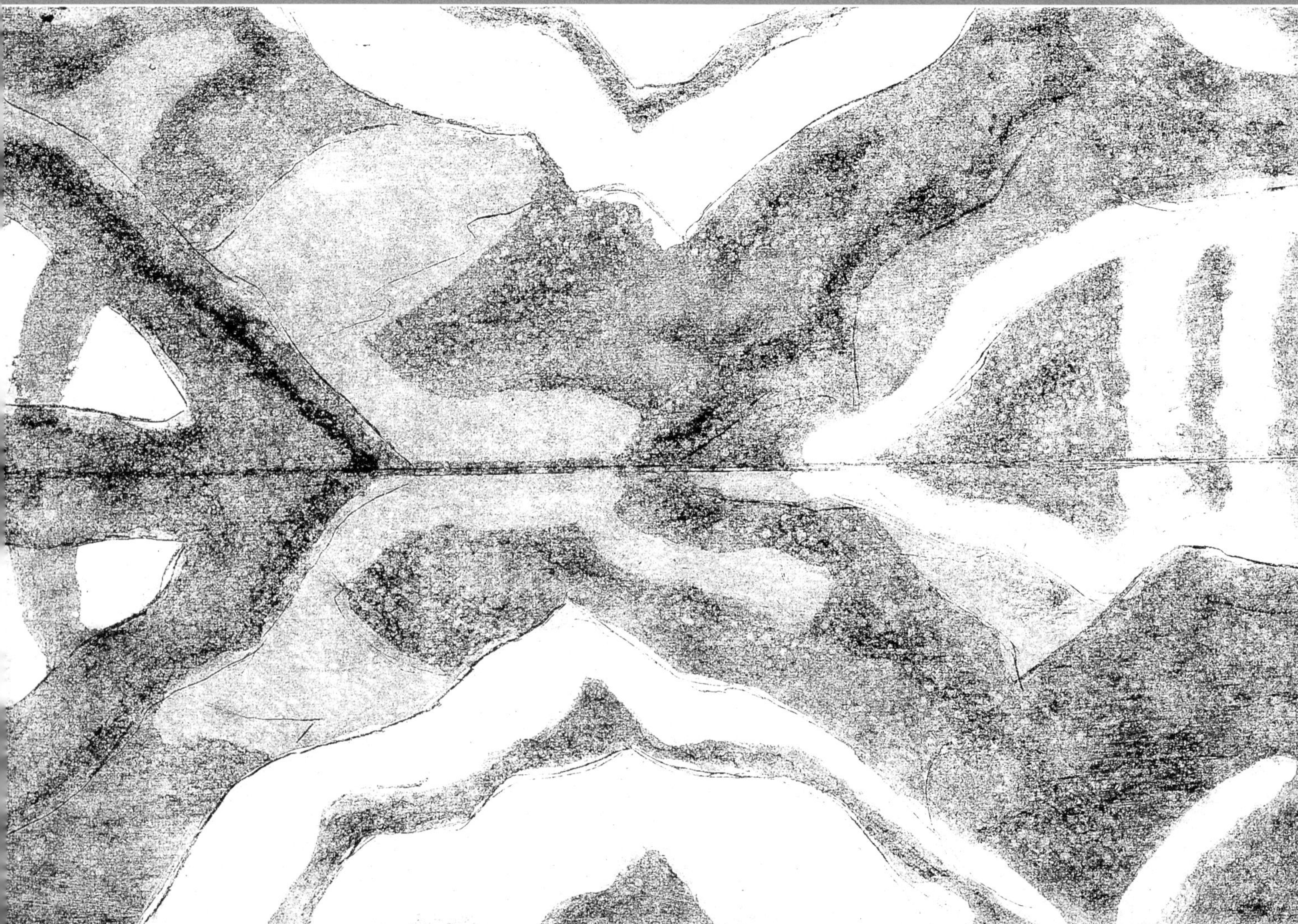

Reflections, intaglio etching, 9⅛ x 5⅞", 1998

The stones are reflections,
reflections of my soul
mirroring the eternity
that I have existed.

They endure, they weather.
They do not resist the forces
which come to change them,
but patiently accept
and slowly change.

Low Tide, drypoint etching, 6 x 8⅝″, 1997

Waking

Morning streaks across my window—
pale grey sky.
Dawn is an early riser.
Light wakes before the birds.

Do they sing with joy?
Are they thankful for the new day?
Do they extol their own magnificence?
Are they letting their friends know
they are still here
and happy to be alive?

Why is it that we don't wake
with a song in our hearts
that we can't contain?

A song just waiting to burst forth
from our lips,
to thank our creator.
Why don't we wake
filled with gratitude and wonder
at being alive,
with the joy
of living another day?

Spirit Wings 2, lino print, $11^{3}/_{4}$ x $8^{7}/_{8}$", 1998

Some nights before the stars
are formed,
intense dark clouds
compress
mountains blacker still.

Likewise, weary flesh and bone
is pressed down,
made numb
by darkness.

But between the mountains and the sky,
a narrow slice
of iridescent green
made from the last gold of sun
touching indigo
awakens heart and eye.

Eyes, heart arise,
awaken
to this fresh splendour.

Night

Through my window
the navy mountain looms,
encased in a pulsing band
of pale green light.

The trees in stark relief
silhouetted against it
and above,
luminous blue,
colour more sumptuous
 each moment.

Nightshades descend.

The Navy Mountain, collage on paper, 20 1/16 x 16 1/16", 2000

Deep metallic blue
dark and shimmery night.
Last kiss of the sun
before the stars spill
their silvery light.

Sheltered

Safe within your arms,
protected from the cold,
wrapped in warmth and light,
I relax, surrender to you.
Supported, I awake,
my courage swells.
Held aloft by your love,
I reach out to try new things,
knowing I am sheltered,
knowing I am home.

Sheltered, acrylic and mixed media on panel, 14½ x 19¼", 1999

The Heart of the Matter, watercolour on paper, 11 3/8 x 15 1/4", 2001

May you have all the joy and success this world has to offer. May you have deep inner peace and contentment. May you have abundant radiant physical, mental, emotional, and spiritual health. May you always work at what you love. May it be play for you. May you feel and know that you are worthy and worthwhile, and that who you are and what you do is making a difference—a real contribution. May you allow your creativity to shine in your work and in countless other ways. May it be a great source of joy and fulfilment to you. May you always have dreams you are working towards and are inspired by. May you always be in a state of becoming.

May you have prosperity and abundance far exceeding your expectations. May you have honest, life-enhancing relations with your family—sharing love, acceptance, and respect. May you feel grateful for your life, for all you have, and for all you are. May you look on the world in wonder and delight in its magnificence each day. May you awake each morning with joyful anticipation for what the day will bring. May you feel the restorative and healing powers of sleep each night. May you experience the joy of continual learning about yourself and your world. May you experience the pleasure of opening and using all of your senses. May you love yourself, treat yourself with compassion and respect, and know the miracle that you are. May you feel love in every cell of your being. May you feel loved and deeply known for who you are—for your essence. May you be so filled to overflowing with love that you easily and generously give it to others and to your world. This is my wish for you. This is my wish for you, and so it is.

About the Works

Knowing, Seeing, Seeds for Thought, A Collection, Inspiration, and *Treasures* are photo etchings from a print collection that I began with the help of Steven Dixon, my printmaking teacher. All were inspired by the poem *Atlin,* written at the Atlin Art Centre in British Columbia. The process entailed making transparencies from enlarged negatives of my photographs and placing them on a special light sensitive film laid over copper plates. The plates set when exposed to light, then were etched in acid, manipulated, and printed. This technique retains a photographic quality in the pieces.

The poems *On a Mountainside, Medicine Wheel, Open Your Senses, Pine Cones, Atlin Lake and Lupine Drops* were also written in Atlin, B.C. The *Mystic Forest Path* was inspired by a walk through Atlin's Mystic Forest—a walk filled with summer flowers and capped by magnificent views of Atlin Lake. Inspiration for the poem *Carol and Me* came in an art therapy exercise that had me go into a painting then explain what was happening inside.

The visual and written works titled *Depression, Release and Clearing, Accept the Moment, Experience,* and *Joy* were written while I sat on the mountain at Atlin. I used them to do a five-part series for one of my drawing courses.

The Dance and *Wild Roses* were both written at Atlin as I smelled the innumerable wild roses and watched the pasque-flower seed heads sway in the wind. Death became more understandable after this latter poem.

The Artist was written at Atlin, and the accompanying artwork titled *The Goddess* is part of a three-part series based on the idea that the Venus of Willendorf is not a fertility figure but a menopausal woman. *She Brings Forth Fruit* is from another three-part series based loosely on the same theme.

The Christ is a poem about a pattern of knots and rings that I see in the cedar wall above my bathtub. Usually my poems preceed the artwork, however, the two prints *Transformation* and *Spirit Wings* came first.

In the fall of 2000, I went to Corsica for an art retreat. My instructor asked that I intently observe the mountain village and decide what attracted me and why. After two days I was asked to narrow my choices to three and determine how they were related. I then wrote a question and a statement about this to inform my future paintings.

I found that dead and dying things, particularly when new life could be seen with the old, were what most attracted me. The next ten days were spent painting the rot in a tree. Each day I would look more closely, enlarging it and observing more deeply. All the while, I kept searching for the light that might be found if I passed through the rot. One day I suddenly asked myself the question, "What if all I find is more rot?" A sobering thought as I realized that I was really delving into the interior parts of myself.

Another morning I noticed that the whole tree trunk was split, not just the area I had been examining. A series of female figures started to appear in my paintings of the space that opened up within the split. *Connected* is one of these. The paintings *Opening, Rot Can Be Beautiful, The Fungus Fairy, Our Fears Are Dragons* and *The Heart of the Matter* owe their origin to the rot in that tree. Eventually I realized that the healthy part of the tree wouldn't be seen if it weren't for the rot giving it texture and contrast, much like life.

After my husband died, I actually experienced the episodes described in *The Floods* in my home. The poem and companion artwork titled *Out of*

Time were inspired by a rhododendron bush that was trying to bloom while there was still snow on the ground. *Hope* and *Sheltered* were done during a Mixed Media course in which I learned that I loved to play in the mud (dry wall compound in this instance). I must not have done enough of this as a child.

The poems *Thank you, Be Careful What You Ask For, His Pain,* and *A Moment in Time* all came to be because a potential love affair went awry. Early morning walks and gazes out my bedroom window inspired the words of *The Collector, Morning Reflections, Reflections, Waking, Dusk, Night,* and *Skybright*. They were written during a creative writing course I took at Capilano College in 1999. The companion creations titled *Web of Life* came into being as I looked up at bare twisting branches one winter morning.

Emerging Depths is my first textile piece. It was made for the "Innovations Show" in Coquitlam, B.C.